Man-Eater

Continued blessings & favor!
Allow God to enlarge your
territory! Greater is coming!

Just S.

.

Printed in the United States of America

ISBN-13: 978-0-578-47342-0

Imprint: JustSReaders

Man-Eater

By Just S.

For all my sister-friends...

"Here's to standing at the top of the stairs and not laying at the bottom." (lol)

Acknowledgments

Where do I begin! I developed a love for writing in fourth grade. Stories became a way of escape and therapy when times were tough. It never got old. It never went bad. Every time I needed to feel better, writing always did the trick. I learned to read and write critically about literature in high school. It soon became a guilty pleasure. I enjoyed writing about reading as much as I enjoyed being a writer. Thank you, Mrs. Maedge for introducing me to the power of a pencil and a notebook. Thank you, Mr. Yoder, for teaching me to think deeply and read with a critical eye.

Every person that ever did anything well, I'm sure had encouragement along the way. Praise and unending support are what I received from my biggest cheerleaders, my parents. Thank you, mom and dad, for your support.

God has always been faithful, even when I didn't deserve it. It is the love of God and His Word that showed me who I am and how much I am worth. Lord, I thank you.

CONTENTS

Introduction

Do you know how easy it is to erase a man from your digital life? It can be done in a matter of seconds if you mean it; every picture, every message, every call, gone just like that. The trail of his existence wiped out at the click of a button.

Don't we all wish he could be erased from our hearts and minds the same way? No remorse. No regret. No looking back. Gone. Just like that. No mental images lingering and hanging around in our inbox. A quick tap on the delete button is all it would take...if it were only that simple.

Where's the app for that?!!

Chapter 1
Breadcrumbs

As an educator, I've learned many strategies for improved student outcomes. The problem is all strategies don't work in all cases with all children. So you have all these tools, and the work comes from having to figure out what you should do to get the best results. As a teacher, you must go into every situation with a plan if you want to experience any amount of success. A rule of thumb is to be reflective and always plan with the end in mind.

In relationships, self-reflection is crucial to future success in dating. If you want the end result of dating to be marriage, then you need to plan for it. Evaluating things that may cause a relationship to be unsuccessful will help you to make decisions that prevent you from repeating cycles that keep you on "Single Street."

We are beginning this journey with the break up because we are going to explore a "backward design" to this whole "man-eating" business. The break up is the end of a failed relationship. The break up is usually dissected and discussed a million times to any girlfriend that will listen. And it is sometimes fabricated to make you look more "victimy" and less "villainy." The reasons for the breakup and the breadcrumbs leading up to it are usually examined and cross-examined by the one friend that insists on playing devil's advocate during your time of pain. (That friend usually goes to timeout for a while so you can decompress and eventually thank her later). So this backward design says, "Hey let's not wait 'til the end to examine the breadcrumbs let's take a look at them now.

Examine your lives as a couple currently. What matches do you have? For example, if spirituality is important to you and it is a guiding force in your life, is it the same for his life? Or if you have satisfied specific requirements that fit your description of a person who is stable enough for a relationship and a potential marriage, does he fit the description too? Does this mean if every aspect of your lives doesn't match then the relationship will fail? No. But it does mean those differences, especially the ones that mean the most to you, are likely to be breadcrumbs if it doesn't work out.

We've all heard the saying, "Communication is the key to successful relationships." So knowing this, why do we ignore or fail to explore a man's communication style early on? Don't answer that question.

What form of communication is needed that makes you most comfortable and secure? Why did I say secure? Insecurity doesn't always set in by being cheated on or mistreated. Sometimes, if you feel there is a lack of communication or the form of communication lacks intimacy, then you might begin to feel insecure about his interest in you and the relationship. Find out sooner than later how he communicates. Is it compatible with your needs? Communication makes all the difference in resolving issues and keeping things moving in a forward motion. Poor communication from the start will undoubtedly be a breadcrumb if not the entire loaf in the end.

Love (or should I say lust) can be blinding, loud, and overshadowing, which makes it hard to read all the signs before commitment. I truly understand why God intended for man and woman to "come together" after marriage, because sex will have wrong feeling right and down feeling up. Crossing those lines before marriage just makes examining breadcrumbs that much more difficult. For instance, how many times have you ignored the fact that he only has time for you on certain days and at certain hours? Did you notice that he has not invited you around the important people in his life? Has he always been too tired when it is time for you to spend time with one another, but when it is something he wants to do he has all the energy in the world? Have you ever wondered about his dreams that don't exactly line up with his work ethic? I mean if you want to be the next millionaire or even a six "figionaire" you can't spend all your time on my couch. When we confuse love with lust, we will make excuses for these behaviors or deny they even exist. We can't make informed decisions when we choose to ignore what we see.

Seeing red flags and not making smart choices about those flags is a crime against you as a person. When you choose to ignore warning signs, you put your peace and your peace of mind in jeopardy. Warnings exist so you can act before it is too late. When we ignore the crumbs on the floor, we end up cleaning up an even larger mess.

The list can go on of all the many things to consider pre-break-up. Examine everything that looks off and feels off from the start. If there is a list of things you want to change right from the beginning, sift through those crumbs. Decide if the crumb is a mere morsel that can easily be digested or is it a heaping pile of beans that may be difficult to chew and swallow.

"When you choose to ignore warning signs, you put your peace and your peace of mind in jeopardy." –Just S.

Your Thoughts Here!

Chapter 2
Ms. Know It All

Hey, I am no expert. But I do know that most people want a chance to talk and be heard. No, I take that back, they really want people to listen to them. When you pick out a watermelon from the grocery store, you try to pick the one that is ripe. The ripe ones are usually the sweetest. You thump it, and you listen for the sound it makes. If you listen carefully and hear a deep hollow sound, that's the one you want. When you listen, you get what you want as a result.

So if you can get what you want from a watermelon by listening, why can't it work for getting what you want from a man? If you want your relationship to have a chance at succeeding, it is necessary to listen to understand not to respond.

Ok, let's stop beating around the bush here. When you come to the table with your strong will, your education, your independence, your ambition, your gross income, and your intellect, it can and potentially will be used against you in a court of love. Is it fair? Is it right? No. It's not fair, and it's not right, but it is real.

What you bring to the table is valuable, but just like any valued thing, when it is misused it is hard to appreciate its worth. No one should be the expert in every situation.

Let me make myself clear. You are worth your weight and more in gold. The hard work and dedication it took to become your phenomenal self; regardless of any relationship (good, bad, or indifferent) is priceless. Staying true to self is critical. Part of being true to who you are is recognizing that becoming a better you involves giving and taking. You have to know when to be the teacher and when to be the learner in a relationship.

Learning involves listening; listening not only with your ears but with your eyes as well. What is it you hear him saying with his lips? What is it you see him saying with his body? As women, we are often very crafty at reading the signs of other women. We practice it. We pride ourselves on it. We can "read" women practically in our sleep. But are we putting to use those same skills when it comes to reading a man? The problem with "Ms. Know It All" is that she often can't "read." She is too busy knowing it

all to see and hear how to approach
certain situations.

Let me offer a little help. You don't have
to know everything all the time.
Sometimes understanding is all that is
required. Sometimes it's necessary to
follow with understanding instead of
leading with knowing. Offering your
support and understanding will help him
come to his own resolutions. You are not
required nor is anyone asking you to
solve a man's problems and all the
problems surrounding the relationship.
Offering your solutions to his issues can
be potentially insulting and annoying. He

knows you are educated and can rule the world if you wanted to, so you don't have to prove it over and over again. He knows that you are a boss or you at least have a boss' mentality that has contributed to your success. He knows that you can work a job, keep a house, take care of the family, and sew on the side all while making dinner. He knows you are a superwoman. Trust me. He's got it!

Some of us are guilty of being know-it-alls. Sometimes it can be seen as endearing and sexy. But let's be real, nobody wants to go ten rounds every argument because no one wants to back down. That gets old, and eventually, someone will want to get out. This character trait is a balancing act. You have to skillfully camouflage your know-it-all ways and work to balance it with learning from others and listening. Does this mean sit back and let the house burn even though you're holding the fire extinguisher? No. It means to allow yourself to be in roles that forge self-directedness in others. Let him come to a resolution on his own with your support. Be a coach, not a consultant!

"You have to skillfully camouflage your know-it-all ways and work to balance it with learning from others and listening."

–Just S.

Coaching involves being an active listener, reading body language, asking thoughtful questions, and using invitational language. Yeah I know it sounds way too deep and like way too much work. But it isn't. Translation: Listen with all your senses, ask questions to show your concern and interest, ask questions to make him think, and be nice about it. Done.

Look I am a recovering or should I say rehabilitating "Ms. Know-It-All." Men have accused me of it on many occasions. At first, I accounted it to insecurity on their part, then jealousy, then just plain ole hateration. Eventually, I had to examine myself. Why do I keep hearing this from people? What is it that I am doing or saying that has made men think this way about me? Ultimately, the only person I can control is myself. If I give myself a once over every now and then, I can make adjustments, tweaks, and alterations to my character that help me to be a better me. Better at listening, better at communicating, better at keeping my finger from waving around when I am being all matter-of-fact, better at keeping my neck still and my eyes less judgy when I speak.

So learn how to test the melon. Yeah, test the melon. He can never accuse you of being a "know it all" if you sit back and listen. Get to know his sound. Listen to him tell you everything that is wrong with the world. And when he's ready, you can coach in and support and challenge him to use the brilliance you know he has to make it better. Get to know his sound. Knowing it will make your relationship that much sweeter.

Reflection is good for the soul!

_____

_____

_____

_____

_____

_____

_____

_____

_____

_____

Chapter 3
Moody Blues

OMG!! Moody men are the worst! It hardly fits the description (at least my description) of a "man." But yes, oh yes men can and will give you the moody blues. Now let's examine this for a minute. What are some things that can put a man in a mood? Work perhaps? He didn't eat lunch? He had to stop and get gas and didn't feel like it? Is he in need of a haircut? I find that men act differently when they are in need of a lining or fade versus when they are not...lol. Dinner

34

was not readily available when he got home, and he is hungry? He has more bills than he has money? Or is he in a mood because of issues with his child's mother? Could it be that you have weekend plans, and he doesn't? Or you had weekend plans last month now you have them again this month? (When will this end he's thinking?) Is he in a mood because his team lost the game, or is it because he didn't even get to watch the game because church service on Sunday ran long? Whatever the reason may be, it has him in a mood. Whatever will you do?

Man moods are so different from woman moods. Man moods will be in full bloom sometimes days before we realize that it is indeed a mood. Now we all have bad days and get a little quiet at times. So naturally we just give one another space, and we are not necessarily checking for a full-on mood swing. With us women folk, you can usually see the switch turn on and off. When we are in a mood, everyone knows almost in advance. Yes, I have been feeling bloated since Tuesday, so I'm guessing by Friday, you should probably stay out of my way. Better yet, just take the weekend, and we will start fresh on Monday. Women moods are different from man moods. The onset of a man mood is subtle almost too subtle to even notice. By the time you realize what is happening you are already entirely annoyed by the mood's existence. You are even more taken aback when you find out that the source and onset of the mood dates back to last month when you had plans for the weekend, and he didn't. Yeah, I'm going to let you ponder on that for a minute.

So yes how men find their way into a mood is different from women. But to keep chaos out of the relationship, there has to be some understanding of what moods are tolerable and those that won't be tolerated. Moodiness can be a deal breaker on either side of the fence. No one wants to be around a Gloomy Gus or a Solemn Suzy. Lack of control of one's mood or emotions can be a more significant issue than you are willing to deal with. But for now, let's set aside the idea of a real medical problem associated with mood swings.

Realistically both men and women will exhibit mood swings. We can't expect men to put up with ours and not even attempt to understand theirs. Even if you feel like man moods are unlike men.

So what do <u>you</u> need when you're feeling moody? Well typically, I'm moody right around that time of the month, so I need baggy clothes, chocolate, tissue to wipe my tears, time, and space. Can this work for men? Tuh, why not?

If a man comes through the door swinging (his mood that is) give him everything you would want and more. He may need to put on his favorite pair of sweats that makes him feel relaxed and free. He may need comfort food to calm his nerves. He may want to spend some time in the bathroom or back porch or in bed to shake it off. We don't want to ignore the mood and be insensitive, but we also don't want to make the mood feel welcomed.

How do we help him to feel better? Allowing him the time, space, and pleasantries he needs to feel better suggests you recognize there is a problem and you care enough to provide things to help put him in a better mood. Sometimes mood swings occur because of misunderstandings, misinterpretations, and lack of mental support in one area or another. You will find that a person can resolve their feelings when they are given the proper time and space to do so. Give him time. Give him space.

Badgering him and making him feel awkward or unmanly for being in his feelings won't make the mood go away. The mood will hang around for a while and eventually just hide until the next time. You want moods related to unresolved feelings and emotions to be dealt with and not covered up. Some of his mood swings will be strictly surface issues that may take food and comfortable clothes to get over. But either way, give him what you would want from someone in the situation and more.

Why more you ask? We have been going through this since we were tweens. We are veterans in the mood game. Men, on the other hand, started swinging right around the time we were granted the right to vote (I kid). Give him space, not grief. We don't always know why we are in a mood. So he may not be able to explain the funk he's in. Don't hover. Treat him like a pie from the oven. It may be hot now, but give it a while to cool. Then it will be just right for tasting.

"*We* don't want to ignore the mood and be insensitive, but we also don't want to make the mood feel welcome."

–Just S.

Your Thoughts Here!

_____

_____

_____

_____

_____

_____

_____

_____

_____

_____

_____

Chapter 4
Support or Sacrifice?

Okay let's be real; we sometimes cross lines in the dating process that shouldn't be crossed. These lines are worse than the ones on a pregnancy test if being pregnant wasn't the plan. There is no such thing as "wifey!" Please do not be deceived. It's wife. W.i.f.e-- wife. A good wife both sacrifices and supports her husband. Sacrifice can be altering her plans and dreams if it means benefiting the marriage and the family. Sacrifice can even be offering up time and money to meet the need of her spouse. Sacrifice is part of marriage, and it is an unspoken commitment that you make when you say, "I do."

Support works the same way as a wife. Wives support their husbands sometimes beyond their means when they need to. Wives support when they don't feel like it. They support when they need support. When you're a wife, it's not one or the other. You will, for the rest of your life, in marital bliss (hopefully) do both. As a wife, you sacrifice and support.

So now let's talk about the rest of us. This next blurb is for all my main chicks, side chicks, weekend chicks, chicks in love with no title, the homey-lover chick, the down a** chick, the he brings me around his family-been around for five years and he still not introducing me as his girlfriend chick, and yes, oh yes the incomparable "wifey chick." Yes, I am talking to you.

How do we get mixed up in these title wars? If the relationship is significant and is purposeful, you will be a girlfriend, a fiancée next, and then a wife. That is the order, always has been. I didn't make it up. It's not my rule. Fight me or deal with it! When we forget this order, we get mixed up and confused with more than just titles and status. We step in and out of roles that we have no business in, and it confuses things more. Stop adding to the confusion by not following the order and doing things that you are not responsible for such as supporting beyond your means and sacrificing beyond recognition.

Who are you? Guess what? If you don't know who you are, it is easy for a man to make you whoever he wants you to be when it suits him. If he needs you to be by his side when he loses a loved one you might be the main chick, but when he is out fishing for catfish, he may want you to be the chick with no title (in other words just a friend). The wifey chick is loyal and is ever present. She has the benefit of his returning home at the end of the night. But what wifey fails to achieve is wife status, which comes with a true, deep commitment on his part. Wifey provides support and sacrifice while getting the stop sign when it comes to marriage. Well, that hardly seems fair. Sometimes wifey chicks are chosen because of all the benefits he can receive without a commitment. His needs exceed his capabilities, and wifey chick makes up for the lack.

So we must take a look at the road that leads us to be deemed something other than girlfriend, fiancée, or wife. How does this happen? To tell you the truth I can't count the ways, but one way is taking on roles and responsibilities that don't belong to us while dating. Dating is a time to get to know one another and grow as a couple. The mystery of each other's separate lives is the thrill of the chase, the element of surprise that keeps the relationship exciting and intriguing. Keeping the balance of togetherness and separateness is important. Too much of one or the other can alter the path of the relationship or ruin it altogether.

The "togetherness" is sometimes how we get ourselves mixed up in a game of titles. We let feelings of being together force a false sense of responsibility when it comes to the man. We start doing things, acting in ways, and taking on roles that are not meant to be present during the dating process. This leads to relationship identity hell where you begin to be confused about who and what you are. And you only find this out when you are denied something that you believe you are entitled to because of who you think you are. You feel jilted when you realize that he does not see you in the way you thought. When you take on responsibilities in dating that you shouldn't, your identity gets mixed up not only to you but to him too. So while we blame the man for not appreciating our worth and what we bring to the table, we must also accept our part in not allowing our worth to be realized in the context in which it should be shown while dating.

I know you're probably thinking but what does all this title business, knowing who you are, and balancing your lives have to do with supporting or sacrificing. Well in a nutshell, if you and the man are not of the mutual understanding of the place, purpose, and direction of your relationship, then you really should hold your sacrifice and support. Why waste it?

I know this may sound hard and you're thinking, "Everybody needs somebody now and then, even if the relationship is murky. We know that life happens, and the presence and support of a significant other can make all the difference in a day gone badly. But we must tread these waters carefully. Bailing him out in ways that cause a lack in your life is called sacrifice. Sacrifices are the duties of a wife. A wife has the commitment from a man to sacrifice for her in return. It's called being married. Without a commitment, sacrifice can be misused and abused. One way to feel taken advantage of after a break-up is to realize how much you sacrificed for someone who never committed to you in that way. Save the sacrifice for after the ceremony.

What about being supportive? Support can be tricky and is not as detrimental as a sacrifice if used with caution. Be supportive with your words and be conscious of your time. Time is too precious to waste. If he could use a kind motivational word in between your decision to move on because you are tired of being the "main" chick, or the "know his family and been around for five years and still don't have a title chick," then go for it. Words are free and they don't make you feel as salty if, and, or when the relationship is over like you would be if you spent thousands of dollars, wasted countless hours, days, years, and risked losing necessities trying to be something called "wifey" that's not even a real thing anyway.

Support is free and part of human nature. Its something you do naturally and something that you shouldn't feel bad about as long as you are supporting positive efforts. Encourage him, offer advice, pray for him, or cheer him on if you wish. But don't waste your time on someone that does not want to spend the time to make things legit with you. Don't get your identity mixed up. Become a girlfriend and never play the role of a wife to someone that's not your husband.

" *I*f you don' t know who you are, it is easy for a man to make you whoever he wants you to be when it suits him. "

—Just S.

Reflection is good for the soul!

_____

_____

_____

_____

_____

_____

_____

_____

_____

_____

_____

Chapter 5
Whose Turn is it?

Playing the numbers game in a relationship and keeping score is "no bueno." It just makes you miserable on the inside when you start adding up how many times you did this, how many times you did that, when you paid for this, so forth and so on. Comparing what you do for him and what he doesn't do for you will end badly.

So how do you deal with feelings of *"what I do for him he does not do for me?"* Answer: You don't have those feelings. Yes, you read the line correctly. You don't have those feelings because what you do for him should be from the heart. What you do for him is not about a return. You give and play your role in a way that keeps you sane no matter the result of the relationship.

There is no such thing as 50/50 all the time. Honestly, I don't think 50/50 exists, (but don't tell anyone I said that). The central message here; fair isn't always equal, and equal isn't always fair. You get what it is. No sense in picking a fight over it. You'll just end up ruining your evening. So please just make peace with it and eat cake, not him.

You must realize that there will be instances where one person (which includes you) might be picking up the slack of the other, but bear in mind that in a relationship (pre-marriage) you absolutely have a choice in the matter. If you believe that the scale has been tipping in his favor for far too long, then choose. Choose not to continue having to overcompensate when he is unable. It is a choice that you have and a choice only you can make. If you begin to feel like your owed a return on what you do, then it's possible you have done too much. Don't do too much.

Now let's be clear, there is a difference between a man not being able to do for his woman and a man not doing for his woman. Know the difference and don't get it twisted. The latter has nothing to do with picking up the slack or an 80/20 split. If a man does not do his reasonable service for a woman while dating, he should not be dating you. If he doesn't realize what his status should be, you better recognize it quickly. Put your fork down, place your napkin on the table, slide your chair out, and get up and walk away as cute as you can.

So let's answer the question! Whose turn is it anyway? This is a tangled web, my friend. I am an old-fashioned girl, and yes I have been raised to presume that the man is the chaser and I am to be chased. I'll also add the idea of when dating the man is supposed to pay. So that means if we date for 1-2 years and go on approximately six hundred twenty-three dates (random figure, these are life lessons, not math lessons) he is supposed to pay for all of them, right? I'm sure that's somehow wrong.

I think us traditionalists have confused being a gentleman and recognizing men as the pursuers with being the cash cow that proves his worthiness by giving up the dough in exchange for the time we spend with them. Exchanging money for time, I'll just leave this here... So once we get past the notion of never having to swipe our card or throw a few dollars on the table we have the sticky web of who's turn is it to pay. Now this may only significantly impact a certain group of ladies because spending money matters to them. For all others, this notion may cause a slight bump in the road to change. So how do we figure this out?

Shall we divide it 50/50? Omg...Are we back to this again?! Please, whatever you do, stay away from math in your relationship. In relationships, numbers tell truths no one wants to know. As a traditionalist, I would offer the advice to allow the man to have first dibs on picking up the check in the beginning. This is a sign of good measure on his part that he would like to provide for you. But this doesn't mean that as an equal measure of good faith you shouldn't offer or insist on picking up the tab every now and then. It is just as crucial for you to show him what you have to offer.

We spin a web of trouble when we try and keep running records of who's doing what. Chances are if you have to keep score, everyone is losing. Or better yet you've already lost. It is possible that you or the guy will carry a little more weight in the relationship at different times. Tracking whether or not the weight is equally distributed is not as important as the weight being carried by whoever has the strength to bear it. This should never be an issue in dating, especially if you're balancing "togetherness " with "separateness." If you are consuming your lives with one another to the point somehow you feel burdened by the expense, you need to check your balance. Dating is not marriage, and as previously stated sacrifices and certain supports are prohibited.

"Chances are if you have to keep score, everyone is losing. Or better yet you've already lost."

—Just S.

Your Thoughts Here!

_____

_____

_____

_____

_____

_____

_____

_____

_____

_____

Chapter 6
Is it me?

Well is it? We ask ourselves this question so many times. But it's odd that we only seem to ask when things are going wrong. When was the last time you were with a guy, and things were going amazingly well, and you wondered, *"Is it me?" "Am I the reason this relationship rocks?"* The answer: never. We only question ourselves in this way when things are not working.

The truth of the matter is, "it takes two to make a thing go right!" (Sure, I'll wait while you finish singing the next part and saying to yourself, that makes even more sense reading it in this book). And more importantly, it takes two to screw it up. We must not carry the burden of failing or failed relationships. We should reflect on and take ownership of our flaws and shortcomings. We all have them. Being imperfect is part of being human. We don't always say the right things, make the best decisions, or select the best partner. Acknowledge that you are imperfect but never take the blame for relationship woes you didn't partake in alone.

The "is it me" complex can be detrimental to future relational situations. It is comparable to low self-esteem, insecurity, and a lack of confidence. And guess what, men can see it a mile away. They can sense the hesitation in your conversation and the moves you make when it comes to being the future "Mrs. Right." Don't let them use this complex as a tool to gain leverage in the relationship.

Realize that dating is a game of chance and risks will be taken. You may not win the first time around. But for lack of a better metaphor, perfect the way you play and stay up on the rules. Dating can be exhausting and striking out gets old. No, it gets depressing. Don't be old or depressing. When men detect your lack of confidence, it is easy to amplify your mistakes to minimize theirs. They have a way of turning a screw up they caused into being your problem. Once you start taking the blame and feeling responsible for the issues in the relationship, it is easy for your confidence to be killed. Keep your confidence. Men like confident women that can be strong, yet vulnerable. Be the woman that makes mistakes and loves who she is while she's making them.

Stop blaming yourself when it doesn't work out. It's not you, and once you believe it, your endless helpings of men can stop. Lose the weight of feeling solely responsible for failed relationships. Then you can go back to fitting those jeans you're trying not to give away.

"When men detect your lack of confidence,

it is easy to amplify your mistakes to

minimize theirs. "

—Just S.

Reflection is good for the soul!

_____

_____

_____

_____

_____

_____

_____

_____

_____

_____

Chapter 7
Come to Jesus

So let me begin by saying, I am not and would not use Jesus' name in vain. Whether you are a believer or not this term means something. Stay with me, we are going somewhere. Jesus is the Son of God, sent down to save us from our sins. He was assigned to carry the weight and the burdens of our past that causes us to be bound by sadness, regret, and un-forgiveness. To come to Jesus would mean to let go off all the mistakes, the pain, hiccups, and hang-ups that cause us to be stagnant and not move forward. To come to Jesus would mean to see the light on a path of darkness, to completely let go of things or thoughts that keep you confused about who you are. Come to Jesus right? If Jesus is the light of the world, then that means anything that is anything is connected to Him in some way. Light is a source of energy, and it provides living things with valuable nutrients. When we "Come to Jesus" we are telling ourselves that I need to get connected to something that gives me life and not death, power and not weakness, success and not failure. Your connection to a source of strength will allow you to break free from relationships, habits of mind, and behaviors that mean you no good. Come to Jesus.

If you are going to move past relationships that caused you pain, caused you to regret your actions, caused you to harbor bitterness and un-forgiveness, caused you to feel unworthy and not good enough, then it would be in your best interest to come to Jesus. Come to a place of light that allows you to see clearly who you are and what you are worth. Let go of the burden of failures in relationships and missteps in love.

Don't allow yourself to be haunted by the ghosts of relationships past. That is not a "Holy Ghost."

Get to a place of peace and solitude to hear and see with clarity your relationship or lack of a relationship. Get to a place of freedom in making decisions about relationships that are best for you. Sometimes not choosing the relationship is the best choice. Don't be afraid to be selective. Look at it, smell it, touch it and then decide if you want it on your plate. Always remember, anything that's blessed won't harm you. So make sure you say grace!

"Come to a place of light that allows you to see clearly who you are and what you are worth."

--Just S.

Your Thoughts Here!

_____

_____

_____

_____

_____

_____

_____

_____

_____

_____

_____

Chapter 8
Man Eater

If you have gotten this far in the text, I hope that the concept of this book is somewhat clear. Be it that I am a novice writer, it might be hopeless. But since you have reached this point, you might as well stay long enough to be let in on what man-eating is all about.

It is nourishing to the body to have a healthy appetite. Eating sparingly causes weakness, malnutrition, and other issues I can't name because I didn't go to medical school. But I know that not eating is unhealthy. We must eat to maintain our strength and keep our mental focus. All food, we know from health class in elementary school, is not good for us. Some foods are better for us than others. Although it may taste good, it is not always good for us, and just because its good for us doesn't mean it has to taste bad. We must try things that are good for us, eliminate things we don't like, and avoid things that are bad for us. I hope I didn't lose you. There is a point. I promise. It's not enough to just eat, but you have to realize what your body needs and what is good. So you have to be "choosy" and ask yourself is this a healthy choice? Healthier food choices help to make your quality of life better, and it makes you feel good. Who doesn't want to feel good? Who doesn't wish to increase their quality of life?

There are choices that you must make to reach health and overall life goals. Having a healthy appetite is not enough. Choosing good foods rich in vitamins and minerals is a responsible decision you must make. Simply eating is a bare minimum. If you want the most from the food you eat, you must control what you eat.

A man-eater is a partaker of men or relationships because of availability, desire, and want with no real endgame or purpose. A man-eater lives at the buffet of "the social scene" snatching and grabbing at whatever looks good. *"Oh, he looks good. Let me waste my time with him." "Oh, he is tall. Let me try him out." "Oooo he is wearing a suit. He seems to be checking for all the ladies tonight, but I'm going to give him my number because I can fix that."* Okay, so these may not exactly be the thoughts going through your head. But you have thoughts, and if you are a man-eater, you're not thinking compatibility is important if this is going to lead to a wedding ceremony. Man-eaters don't ask, "Why are we dating?" Man-eaters can't answer, "Are we committed?" Man-eaters don't know the relationship goals. These are questions you should be able to answer and information you should know if you are doing it right.

Sometimes you can be light years ahead of a man in a relationship and wonder why you are suddenly not clicking with one another. It is because you never stopped to establish (together) what you both want short term and long term as it relates to the relationship. Or you may not be clicking because you thought you established what you both wanted but did not align his actions with his words to determine a disconnect.

Man-eaters have countless relationships and pour their hearts out countless numbers of times over and over again, without stopping to reflect. And I don't mean thinking about how you miss him, how sad you are because it didn't work, whose fault it is, why it's his fault and not your fault, or it's your fault but mostly his fault. None of that, I mean truly stopping to reflect deeply about eating before you choose and choosing before you eat.

Choosing before you eat is a product of deep reflection. Asking yourself critical questions before, during, and after relationships will curb the man-eating appetite. What matches do or did we have? Is spirituality a guiding force in his life like it is in mine? Does he or has he satisfied specific requirements that fit my description of a person who is stable enough for a relationship and possible marriage? Is his communication style compatible with my needs? Don't just eat something because it's in front of you. Ask to see the menu. Ask about the soup of the day. Ask about the specials. And know where the fish came from. A man-eater reformed will be well informed and choose their next meal wisely.

"A man-eater is a partaker of men or relationships because of availability, desire, and want with no real endgame or purpose."

—Just S.

Reflection is good for the soul!

_____

_____

_____

_____

_____

_____

_____

_____

_____

_____

Chapter 9
Waiting

Why must we wait? Why is waiting sometimes just as painful as relationships themselves? When will my plus one arrive? How long will it take? What do I need to do to speed up this process? Let me tell you something about waiting. Waiting is the one thing in life that no matter what is going on, you have zero control over the time. For example, when you are scheduled to meet friends at seven p.m., and they don't show up until whatever time they decide to get there, you have no control over the time you wait for them. Leaving and going home doesn't count because that would mean you have abandoned the objective of getting together. When you make an appointment to see the doctor at two p.m., and he doesn't get to you until an hour later, you, my friend are at the mercy of whatever time the door swings open, and your name is called. You are not in control. Waiting means you have no control, say so, or resolution to what is happening. If you had that kind of power, then you would not be waiting. So your soul mate's entrance into your life is not up to you. You don't get to decide, hence the waiting.

The worst part about being single but wanting to be married is waiting. What am I doing while I'm waiting? Not dating while waiting is the craziest thing I have ever heard in my life. How the heck do you expect to get "wifed up" without getting out there? My opinion (and no one asked for it) date, but don't serial date.

Serial dating is dating out of control; dating just to be dating. It's random with no real purpose. You are dating but not dating anyone long enough or thoughtfully enough to have a real chance at something special. That's serial dating. Don't serial date.

And don't believe the hype when you hear people say, "You need to date to know what you like." You know you better than anyone breathing. So it's not a matter of finding out what you want or like. If you don't know that going in, then you should not be dating anyone. (Stop ruining people's lives because you don't know what you want). Get yourself together before you involve others (I went off, but I still love you).

Getting out there may start off as innocent flirting, conversation, and casual company but lead to more serious relationships and serious commitments.

This is tricky for two reasons. Chasing slacks could never end well. I'm sorry I just don't see it. Men by nature are hunters, and they want to hunt and pursue. So if "getting out there" involves you initiating the courtship, then you can almost count on initiating many other things in the relationship...to eaches own on this one.

Reason number two; dating around can lead to "man-eater" like ways. You know, going in and out of relationships trying to make it happen but no clue on what making it happen is. Dating men that you feel you have to "work on" (and it ends in ruins) pushes you on to the next "project" if you don't check your "man-eater tendencies." Constantly going into relationships to fill the hole in your heart will only make the hole bigger and deeper. A "man-eater" ignores how the hole got there and just keeps trying to fill it no matter what. Dating should not be used as a filler.

Dating men to occupy your time, while you wait for "Mr. Right," is like doing crossword puzzles at the DMV. Here's the danger in doing crossword puzzles while waiting; there is a chance that while you are searching for the word atmosphere, you may not realize that your number popped up on the screen, and you miss your turn. There is a chance while you're leaning over to ask the person next to you "what's a four letter word for someone who is homeless" and share a laugh because you feel silly for not knowing the word was "hobo" you may not hear your name called. Waiting and having something to do definitely can get you by, but it doesn't do much else. Think of how mentally exhausted you might be searching for hundreds, thousands of words with no respect of time. Just think of how much eating you can do with no constraints or limits. And think of how full you may be when you get to your final plate. When "mister" finally makes his entrance will you be okay with the effects of your habits while waiting? He has come into the picture, but are you at your best after all those calories? Think about it.

And for those traditional women, spiritual women, the good book says, "He that finds a wife..." So this tells us in so few words to wait. As difficult as it might be, this one line sums it up. To be found, you must first be lost. And something lost is what: waiting to be found. Be lost to giving yourself away to those that don't deserve you. Be lost to temporarily satisfying physical needs. Be lost to giving up your greatness to just be good enough. If you do these things, you can rest assured that (someday) when it's cold outside, and the sky, covered with thick dreary clouds, and the rain is falling from every direction, which makes it hard to see, there will be a ray of sunshine unexpectedly.

The sudden beautiful break in the clouds and the rain passing through is guaranteed. Rain does not come to stay, and neither does the waiting period. Someday the unexpected will happen. The sudden tap on your shoulder, the sudden look from across the room, the unexpected "pardon me" at the grocery store in an aisle full of ripe, sweet melons, is going to happen. Just you wait and see!

"Dating should not be used as a filler." –Just S.

Your Thoughts Here!

_____

_____

_____

_____

_____

_____

_____

_____

_____

_____

About the Author

Just S. is an accomplished leader in education. Born and raised in St. Louis, MO she has served in the public school sector in various leadership roles for more than ten years. She is active in her local ministry and a believer in the power of prayer. You will come to love and appreciate her honesty, humor, and the way she tells it like it is when it comes to relationships, living life, and personal growth.

TALES FROM "THE CAT"

(A snippet from Book #2 *Man-Eater: The Sex Chapters*)

Ok, this next part may take some by storm. For my Christian women, according to the Holy Bible, having sex before marriage is not an option. But let's keep it real, there are a number of us (and I do mean a substantial number of us) that do not uphold or live up to the charge of abstaining without fail. So tell the truth. You are doing it or you have done it! As for everyone else sex is likely happening in your relationships regularly. So what's wrong with doing it?

Having sex and trying to solidify a genuine, deep connection with a man is difficult. It is difficult because sex satisfies a psychological desire that manifests itself physically. So two significant parts of you are consumed by having sexual encounters with the men you date. Sex has a way of changing the shade of a relationship. Sex can make it look green, but in reality, it's been red from the beginning.

Where does sex fall on your list of things necessary in a successful relationship? Do your beliefs change depending on the relationship? Exactly how much power does the p#$$y have? Is "she" more powerful than you? Eventually, we will examine abstaining versus not abstaining, but not just yet. Before you decide whether sex is a must when dating, a better question to ask yourself might be "If my precious punani could talk, what would it say about me?"

So you're either laughing out loud at the thought of what "she" might say or you are feeling uncomfortable and relieved that "she" can never tell her truth concerning your past. Either way, thinking about how and what sex has meant to your physical and spiritual being is an essential step in not letting history repeat itself.

*"**Sex** has a way of changing the shade of a relationship."—Just S.*

Want to read more? Stay connected for the release
of Man-eater: The Sex Chapters by Just S.

Follow the author's blog on Facebook:
Kitten Heel Chronicles
@TheKittenHC or fb.me/TheKittenHC

email:
justsreaders@gmail.com

Your Thoughts Here!

_____

_____

_____

_____

_____

_____

_____

_____

_____

_____

_____

Your Thoughts Here!

_____

_____

_____

_____

_____

_____

_____

_____

_____

_____

_____

Your Thoughts Here!

_____

_____

_____

_____

_____

_____

_____

_____

_____

_____

_____

Your Thoughts Here!

_____

_____

_____

_____

_____

_____

_____

_____

_____

_____

Made in the USA
Columbia, SC
24 May 2019